Guide to Eclipse VIATRA

Practical Guide

V. Telman

Copyright © 2024

Practical Guide

1.Introduction to Eclipse VIATRA

What is Eclipse VIATRA?

Eclipse VIATRA (VIATRA Model Query and Transformation Framework) is a powerful development framework that enables the transformation and manipulation of models in model-based software systems (Model-Driven Engineering, MDE). VIATRA is integrated into the Eclipse platform and supports a wide range of functionalities for querying, transforming, and validating models, making it a fundamental tool in areas like automated code generation, property verification, and model synchronization.

VIATRA is based on an efficient query engine, designed to handle complex and large models with high performance. It can operate in both batch mode (executing queries once on a static model) and incremental mode (where queries are continuously executed as the model is updated). This flexibility makes it suitable for various scenarios, such as automating software engineering tasks, model evolution, change tracking, and more.

The VIATRA framework is built on two main components:

1. **VIATRA Query**: A library that provides a declarative query language to retrieve information from models.

2. **VIATRA Transformation**: A transformation engine that allows for the specification of bidirectional transformations, which can be used to synchronize different models.

Main Features

Eclipse VIATRA offers a broad set of features that make it highly useful in various contexts related to model manipulation and transformation:

1. **Incremental Query Engine**

The VIATRA query engine can update query results incrementally. This means that once a query is executed, the engine can automatically update the results based on changes made to the model, without recalculating the query from scratch. This incremental approach is highly valuable for real-time systems, where rapid response to model changes is required.

2. **Bidirectional Transformations**

The ability to define bidirectional transformations allows VIATRA to keep two distinct models synchronized. This is particularly useful in contexts where there are different representations of the same system, such as a conceptual model and an implementation model, and where it is important that changes in one model are automatically reflected in the other.

3. **Support for Verification and Validation Methods**

VIATRA provides a set of tools for model verification and validation, allowing developers to ensure that a model satisfies certain formal properties. Thanks to its integration with the query engine, it is possible to continuously verify the model as it evolves, ensuring that all changes comply with the established rules.

4. **Integration with Other Eclipse Technologies**

As part of the Eclipse ecosystem, VIATRA easily integrates with other modeling and development tools available on the platform, such as EMF (Eclipse Modeling Framework), Xtext, Papyrus, and many others. This makes it ideal for complex projects that require the integration of multiple tools and technologies.

5. **Declarative Query Language**

VIATRA uses a declarative query language, similar to SQL, that allows developers to write queries in an intuitive and readable manner. This language supports logical operators, aggregate functions, and many other useful constructs for expressing complex queries on models.

6. **Efficient Transformation Execution**

Thanks to the optimized architecture of the query and transformation engine, VIATRA ensures efficient execution even with large-scale models. This makes the framework suitable for complex industrial systems and for processing models that may contain millions of elements.

Advantages of Using VIATRA

Using Eclipse VIATRA offers numerous advantages, especially for developers working in the context of model-driven engineering:

1. **Efficiency and Performance**

The incremental query engine saves

computational resources by not requiring complete recalculation of queries in response to model changes. This ensures rapid system response, even with large-scale models.

2. **Automation of Transformations**

With VIATRA, many common model manipulation tasks, such as code generation, constraint verification, or model synchronization, can be automated. This helps reduce errors and improve productivity.

3. **Continuous Verification**

Thanks to its support for model verification and validation, developers can quickly identify any violations of rules or constraints during development, thus improving software quality.

4. **Ease of Integration**

VIATRA integrates seamlessly with other Eclipse tools, simplifying its adoption in existing development environments. This reduces integration costs and allows VIATRA to be used in conjunction with technologies like EMF and GMF.

5. **Support for Bidirectional Transformation**

The ability to synchronize different models bidirectionally is particularly useful in complex projects where consistency between multiple views or representations of the system is crucial.

Installing Eclipse VIATRA

To start using Eclipse VIATRA, certain installation and configuration steps are required, including downloading the development environment, configuring Eclipse, and installing the VIATRA plugins.

System Requirements

Before proceeding with the installation of Eclipse VIATRA, it's important to ensure that your system meets the following minimum requirements:

1. **Operating System**

VIATRA is compatible with the following major operating systems:

- Windows 10 or higher

- macOS 10.14 (Mojave) or higher

- Linux distributions based on kernel 4.15 or higher (e.g., Ubuntu 18.04 or newer)

2. **Java Version**

Eclipse VIATRA requires a Java Runtime Environment (JRE) or Java Development Kit (JDK) version 11 or higher. It is recommended to install a JDK to develop and run projects involving VIATRA.

3. **Memory**

For smooth use of Eclipse VIATRA, at least 8 GB of RAM is recommended. However, for complex projects or very large models, it is advisable to have at least 16 GB of RAM to ensure optimal performance.

4. **Disk Space**

Installing Eclipse and the related plugins requires at least 1 GB of free disk space. If you plan to work with very large models or numerous plugins, it is preferable to have at least 2-3 GB of available space.

5. **Internet Connection**

Although Eclipse can function offline, an internet connection is required to download the Eclipse package and necessary plugins, including future updates.

Download and Configuration

1. **Download Eclipse IDE**

The first step in installing VIATRA is to download the Eclipse IDE. To do so:

- Visit the official Eclipse website (https://www.eclipse.org/downloads/).

- Select the Eclipse IDE for Java Developers version, as this includes support for Java development, which is necessary for using VIATRA.

- Choose the appropriate package for your operating system (Windows, macOS, Linux) and proceed with the download.

2. **Install Eclipse**

Once the installation file is downloaded, proceed with the installation:

- On **Windows**, run the downloaded installer (e.g., `eclipse-inst-jre-win64.exe`) and follow the on-screen instructions to install Eclipse.

- On **macOS**, mount the `.dmg` file and drag the Eclipse icon into the `Applications` folder.

- On **Linux**, extract the downloaded `.tar.gz` archive into a folder and launch Eclipse by running the `eclipse` script from the extracted directory.

3. **Configure Eclipse**

After completing the installation, open Eclipse and select a workspace, which will be the folder where your projects will be saved. You will then be greeted with the main Eclipse IDE screen, where you can begin working. Before moving on to the installation of VIATRA, it is helpful to configure some basic parameters to optimize the development environment:

- **Allocated Memory**: Adjust the Eclipse configuration to allocate more memory if needed. This can be done by modifying the `eclipse.ini` file (in the Eclipse installation directory), increasing the `-Xms` (minimum memory) and `-Xmx` (maximum memory) values to avoid performance issues.

For example:

```
-Xms512m
-Xmx4096m
```

- **Installing Java JDK**: If you haven't already, ensure that Eclipse is using the correct version of the JDK. Go to *Window* > *Preferences* > *Java* > *Installed JREs* and select the desired JDK.

2. Fundamental Concepts of Eclipse VIATRA

Eclipse VIATRA is a powerful and flexible platform for model management and transformation in Model-Driven Engineering (MDE). Used in various software development contexts, VIATRA allows for model querying, automatic transformations, and property verification. With an efficient pattern matching engine and a declarative query language, VIATRA is particularly useful for those working with complex models and needing to automate intricate operations.

In this overview, we will explore VIATRA's fundamental concepts, focusing on:

- **Models and Metamodels**

- **Transformation Rules**

- **Pattern Matching**

Each of these concepts will be accompanied by detailed explanations and practical examples to provide a comprehensive understanding of VIATRA.

Models and Metamodels

Concept of a Model

In Eclipse VIATRA, as in other model-driven platforms, a **model** represents an abstract description of a system or domain. A model consists of objects and relationships that capture specific aspects of a system, such as classes, attributes, associations, and behaviors.

For example, in a university management system context, a model might represent entities like **Student**, **Course**, and **Professor**, along with their relationships, such as student enrollment in courses or the assignment of professors to specific courses.

Concept of a Metamodel

A **metamodel** defines the structure and

constraints for a set of models. It is essentially a "model of models," specifying the rules by which concrete models can be constructed. For instance, if a model represents a university management system, the metamodel defines which entities can exist (e.g., Student, Course, Professor), the attributes these entities can have, and the types of relationships allowed between them.

A common example of a metamodel is **Ecore**, the metamodel underlying the **Eclipse Modeling Framework (EMF)**. Ecore defines how to create and manage domain models in Eclipse, with concepts like **EClass** (representing a class), **EAttribute** (representing a class attribute), and **EReference** (representing a relationship between classes).

Example of Model and Metamodel

Imagine creating a model to represent a university management system. Our metamodel defines the following entities and relationships:

- **Class "Student"** with attributes "name" and "enrollment number."

- **Class "Course"** with attributes "title" and "code."

- **Class "Professor"** with an attribute "name."

- **Relationship "enrolled_in"** that connects a student to one or more courses.

- **Relationship "teaches"** that connects a professor to one or more courses.

The metamodel establishes that these entities and relationships are valid and defines the rules by which they can be instantiated. A concrete model based on this metamodel could include:

- The student "Mario Rossi" (enrollment number: 12345) is enrolled in the course "Mathematics" (code: MAT101).

- Professor "Dr. Bianchi" teaches the course "Mathematics."

Models in VIATRA

In VIATRA, models are represented using the EMF framework. Developers can define Ecore metamodels using Eclipse modeling tools and then create instances of these models to query or transform using VIATRA.

Creating an EMF Model

Suppose we want to create a simple model representing a company with employees and projects. We can define an Ecore metamodel as follows:

- **Class "Employee"** with attributes "name" (string) and "ID" (integer).

- **Class "Project"** with attributes "name" (string) and "budget" (integer).

- **Relationship "assigned_to"** that connects one or more employees to one or more projects.

Once the metamodel is defined, we can create model instances (employees and projects) using EMF tools, and then query or transform them using VIATRA.

Transformation Rules

Concept of Transformation

A **transformation** in VIATRA is an operation that takes a model as input and produces another model (or modifies the existing one) as output. Transformations can be unidirectional (where the target model is generated from the source model) or bidirectional (where changes in one model are automatically reflected in the other).

Transformation rules in VIATRA are defined using a declarative language based on pattern matching. A transformation rule specifies the conditions under which a part of the model should be transformed and describes the action to be taken when those conditions are met.

Defining Transformation Rules

A transformation rule in VIATRA consists of two parts:

- **Left-hand side (LHS)**: Describes the pattern that must be found in the source model. This is a declarative description of a configuration of objects that must meet certain conditions.

- **Right-hand side (RHS)**: Describes the actions that should be performed once the pattern is found. These actions can include creating new objects, modifying attributes, or creating new relationships between objects.

Example of a Transformation Rule

Suppose we want to automate the creation of a project for each employee not yet assigned to any project. We can define a transformation rule as follows:

1. **LHS (Pattern Matching)**: Find all "Employee" objects not assigned to any project (i.e., no relationship exists between the employee and a project).

2. **RHS (Action)**: Create a new "Project" object and assign the employee found to this new project.

Writing a Transformation Rule in VIATRA

In VIATRA, transformation rules are defined using the VIATRA transformation language, which is based on pattern matching. Here's an example of a simple transformation rule:

```java
rule AssignEmployeeToProject {
    // LHS: find an employee without projects
    from employee : Employee
    where {
        not find EmployeeAssignedToProject(employee);
    }
    // RHS: create a new project and assign the employee
```

```
    to {
        var newProject = new Project;
        employee.assigned_to = newProject;
    }
}
```

In this example:

- The **LHS** uses a pattern to find an employee who is not yet assigned to a project.

- The **RHS** creates a new project and assigns the found employee to the project.

Executing Transformations

Once a transformation rule is defined, VIATRA executes the transformation by searching for patterns in the source model and applying the specified actions in the RHS. Transformations can be executed in batch mode (one-time execution) or in incremental mode, where the transformation is automatically applied whenever the model changes.

Practical Example

Let's say we have a model representing a company with employees and projects. Initially, we have the following data:

- Employee "Mario Rossi" (ID: 1001) is not assigned to any project.

- Employee "Giulia Bianchi" (ID: 1002) is assigned to Project "A."

After executing the transformation rule we defined, VIATRA will create a new project for Mario Rossi and assign him to that project. The updated model might look like this:

- Employee "Mario Rossi" (ID: 1001) is assigned to Project "NewProject1."

- Employee "Giulia Bianchi" (ID: 1002) is assigned to Project "A."

Pattern Matching

Concept of Pattern Matching

Pattern matching is a core concept in Eclipse VIATRA and refers to the system's ability to search for and identify specific configurations of objects and relationships within a model. Essentially, a "pattern" describes a set of conditions that model elements must meet, and the pattern-matching engine finds all instances of that pattern present in the model. Pattern matching underpins both querying and transformations in VIATRA, as it allows users to identify parts of the model to perform operations on.

In VIATRA, patterns are expressed using the **Viatra Query Language (VQL)**, a declarative language that allows flexible and simple definition of the conditions that must be met to locate pattern instances within the model.

Defining Patterns in VIATRA

A pattern in VIATRA can be viewed as a "question" posed to the model: "Which elements satisfy these conditions?" Each pattern consists of a set of **variables** (representing model objects) and a series of **constraints** these variables must satisfy (e.g., relationships between objects or attribute conditions).

Basic Pattern Syntax

Here's an example of a pattern written in Viatra Query Language (VQL) that finds all employees in a company:

```vql
pattern allEmployees(employee: Employee) {
    Employee(employee);
}
```

This pattern looks for all objects of type `Employee` within the model and associates them with the `employee` variable. The condition to satisfy this pattern is simply that the object must be of type `Employee`.

Complex Patterns

Patterns in VIATRA can become much more complex, involving multiple variables and constraints. For example, we can search for employees assigned to a specific project:

```vql
pattern employeeAssignedToProject(employee: Employee, project: Project) {
    Employee(employee);
    Project(project);
    employee.assigned_to(project);
```

}
```

In this case, the pattern looks for a pair of objects, an `Employee` and a `Project`, and verifies that there is a relationship between them (the employee is assigned to the project).

### Using Attributes in Patterns

In addition to relationships between objects, you can also define constraints on the attributes of objects. For example, to find all employees with a specific ID:

```vql
pattern employeeByID(employee: Employee, id: Int) {

   Employee(employee);

   employee.ID == id;

    }
    ```

This pattern finds employees whose `ID` attribute matches the value provided in the `id` variable.

Hierarchical and Reusable Patterns

In VIATRA, patterns can be composed, meaning one pattern can invoke other patterns. This allows for the creation of modular and reusable pattern definitions. For example, a pattern that finds all employees can be used as a building block in another pattern that finds employees assigned to a specific project.

Example:

```vql

```
pattern employeesInProject(project: Project, employee: Employee) {
    find allEmployees(employee);
    employee.assigned_to(project);
}
```

In this case, the `employeesInProject` pattern uses the previously defined `allEmployees` pattern to identify employees, then adds an additional constraint that the employee must be assigned to the specified project.

Benefits of Pattern Matching in VIATRA

The pattern-matching engine in VIATRA is highly optimized for large and complex models. Some of its key benefits include:

- **Efficiency**: VIATRA uses advanced algorithms to quickly find pattern instances, even in large models.

- **Incrementality**: In many cases, VIATRA can update its pattern-matching results incrementally, meaning that changes to the model trigger only small, localized updates to the pattern-matching results. This is especially useful in interactive or real-time applications where the model is constantly changing.

Eclipse VIATRA is a versatile and efficient tool for managing models and executing complex transformations in Model-Driven Engineering. By providing powerful features for querying models using pattern matching and automating transformations based on predefined rules, VIATRA enables developers to create dynamic and adaptable systems.

The core concepts of **models and metamodels**, **transformation rules**, and **pattern matching** form the foundation of VIATRA. Through practical examples, we have seen how these concepts can be applied to real-world scenarios, such as assigning employees to projects or managing university systems.

Mastering these fundamentals will empower you to leverage VIATRA in various model-driven development tasks, from querying and analyzing models to automating transformations and synchronizing different model views.

3. Using Eclipse VIATRA

Eclipse VIATRA allows developers to define metamodels, execute transformations, and automate complex operations on models, simplifying the management of complex and dynamic projects. In this guide, we will explore how to use VIATRA practically and in detail, focusing on:

- Creating VIATRA projects
- Defining metamodels
- Writing transformation rules

Each section will be enriched with practical examples to provide a concrete and operational understanding of how to use VIATRA in software development.

Creating Projects in Eclipse VIATRA

Steps for Creating a Project in VIATRA

Creating a project in Eclipse VIATRA follows a series of standard steps. Here's a detailed guide on how to create a VIATRA project from scratch:

1. Creating an EMF Project

VIATRA is based on the Eclipse Modeling Framework (EMF), so the first step is to create an EMF project, which will serve as the foundation for models and transformations.

- **Step 1:** Open Eclipse and select **File → New → Project...**
- **Step 2:** Choose **Ecore Modeling Project** from the list of available projects and click **Next**.
- **Step 3:** Name the project, e.g., `UniversityModel`, and select the destination folder.

- **Step 4:** Configure the EMF project settings as required and click **Finish**.

This will create the basic structure of an EMF project, including a `model` folder where the Ecore metamodel file will be stored.

2. Defining the Ecore Model

After creating the EMF project, the next step is to define the Ecore metamodel, which represents the model's structure. An example of a metamodel for a university system might include entities like Students, Courses, and Professors.

- **Step 1:** Right-click on the `model` folder and select **New → Ecore Diagram** to create a new Ecore model file.
- **Step 2:** In the Ecore diagram, add the following classes:

    - **Student** with attributes `name` (String)

and `id` (int)

  - **Course** with attributes `title` (String) and `code` (String)

  - **Professor** with the attribute `name` (String)

- **Step 3:** Define relationships between the classes. For example, you can define a `reference` relationship called `enrolledIn` linking `Student` to `Course`, and a relationship called `teaches` connecting `Professor` to `Course`.

Once the Ecore metamodel is created, you'll have a `.ecore` file in the project that represents the conceptual structure of your system.

3. Integrating VIATRA

With the Ecore metamodel defined, you can now add support for VIATRA to the project.

- **Step 1:** Right-click on the project and select **Configure → Add VIATRA Nature**. This will enable VIATRA support for the project.

- **Step 2:** Configure the necessary VIATRA dependencies, including the VIATRA Query and Transformation plugins, which will allow you to define queries and transformation rules.

At this point, your project is ready to host VIATRA transformations and queries.

Creating Pattern Matching Queries

After configuring the project, you can begin writing pattern matching queries to query the model. These queries are written using the declarative Viatra Query Language (VQL).

Here's an example of a query that finds all students enrolled in a specific course:

```vql
pattern studentsInCourse(student: Student, course: Course) {
    Student(student);
    Course(course);
    student.enrolledIn(course);
}
```

This query searches the model for all instances of students enrolled in a course and can be executed to get the desired results.

Defining Metamodels

What is a Metamodel?

A **metamodel** is a formal description of

the structure of a model. In Eclipse VIATRA, the metamodel is defined using Ecore, which is the metamodel underlying the Eclipse Modeling Framework (EMF). A metamodel specifies entity types, their properties, and relationships between them.

Example of a University Metamodel

To better understand how metamodels work in VIATRA, consider an example of a metamodel representing a university management system. Such a metamodel might include the following entities and relationships:

- **Student**: has the attributes `name` (String) and `id` (Integer).

- **Course**: has the attributes `title` (String) and `code` (String).

- **Professor**: has the attribute `name` (String).

- **`enrolledIn` Relationship**: represents a

student's enrollment in one or more courses.

- **`teaches` Relationship**: represents the professor teaching one or more courses.

Creating an Ecore Metamodel in VIATRA

Here are the steps to create a metamodel in Ecore:

1. **Define the main classes**: Create the main classes (Student, Course, Professor) and assign appropriate attributes to each of them.

2. **Define the relationships**: Add relationships between the classes using references. For example, the `enrolledIn` relationship between `Student` and `Course` is a many-to-many reference connecting multiple students to multiple courses.

3. **Set constraints**: Constraints can be added to models to specify further structural rules, such as the cardinality of relationships (e.g., a student can be enrolled in many courses, but a course must have at least one student).

Example Model

After defining the metamodel, you can create a concrete instance of the model. For example:

- **Student "Mario Rossi"** (id: 12345)
- **Course "Mathematics"** (code: MAT101)
- **Professor "Dr. Bianchi"**

Mario Rossi is enrolled in the Mathematics course, which is taught by Dr. Bianchi. This represents a concrete instance of the model based on the structure defined by the metamodel.

Writing Transformation Rules

The Concept of Transformation

Transformations are operations that modify a source model to generate a target model or make changes to the same model. In VIATRA, transformation rules are defined using pattern matching to find specific parts of the model and then perform actions to transform them.

Structure of a Transformation Rule

A transformation rule in VIATRA consists of two main parts:

1. **LHS (Left-Hand Side)**: Defines the pattern that needs to be found in the model.

2. **RHS (Right-Hand Side)**: Defines the

action to perform when the pattern is found. This action can include creating new objects, modifying attributes, or creating new relationships between objects.

Example of a Transformation Rule

Let's consider an example where we want to automatically create a project for each employee not assigned to a project.

- **LHS**: Find all employees who are not yet assigned to any project.

- **RHS**: Create a new project and assign the employee to the new project.

The rule can be defined as follows:

```java
rule assignEmployeeToProject {
```

```
// LHS: find unassigned employees
from employee: Employee
where {
    not find employeeAssignedToProject(employee);
}
// RHS: create new project and assign employee
to {
    var newProject = new Project;
    employee.assignedTo(newProject);


    // Set some attributes of the new project, such as a default title
    newProject.title = "Project Assigned to " + employee.name;
    newProject.code = "PROJ-" + employee.id;
  }
}
```

Using Eclipse VIATRA allows you to efficiently and flexibly manage and manipulate complex models. Through:

- **Project creation**, including defining models and metamodels,

- **Writing transformation rules** to automate changes and object creation in the model,

- **Pattern matching** to identify specific structures in models,

VIATRA presents itself as a powerful tool in model-driven engineering.

4.Integration with Eclipse VIATRA

Eclipse VIATRA is a powerful tool for model transformation and pattern matching, but its true strength is revealed when properly integrated with the Eclipse workspace. This integration enables developers to fully leverage VIATRA's features, particularly the ability to create a customized development environment, customize tools, and use debugging tools to address complex issues related to transformations and queries.

In this article, we will explore how to efficiently integrate VIATRA with Eclipse, focusing on three key areas:

1. **Workspace Setup**

2. **Customizations**

3. **Debugging Tools**

Each section will include practical examples

and tips on how to configure and optimize Eclipse for VIATRA, with a focus on creating an effective development environment.

---

1. Workspace Setup

Configuring the Workspace for VIATRA

To fully leverage VIATRA's capabilities, the workspace within Eclipse must be correctly configured. VIATRA requires specific dependencies, such as the Eclipse Modeling Framework (EMF), and supporting tools for model and transformation management.

1.1. Installing Eclipse and VIATRA

Before proceeding with VIATRA integration,

ensure you have installed Eclipse and all necessary components. Here's a brief guide on how to install VIATRA in Eclipse:

1. **Download and Install Eclipse Modeling Tools**: VIATRA is integrated into the "Eclipse Modeling Tools" package, which includes all the plugins necessary for working with models and metamodels. You can download it from [eclipse.org](https://www.eclipse.org/downloads/).

2. **Install VIATRA**:

   - Launch Eclipse.

   - Go to **Help → Eclipse Marketplace**.

   - In the search bar, type **VIATRA** and select the **VIATRA Framework** plugin.

   - Click **Install** and follow the instructions to complete the installation.

3. **Verify Installation**: After installing VIATRA, verify that the plugin is correctly

configured by checking if the **VIATRA Query Development** and **VIATRA Transformation** menus are available in Eclipse's toolbar.

1.2. Organizing the Workspace

The Eclipse workspace is customizable and modular, allowing you to organize the interface according to your workflow needs. Here are some tips for setting up your workspace for VIATRA development:

- **Modeling Perspective**: Eclipse offers various perspectives for different project types. For projects using VIATRA, it is recommended to use the **Modeling** perspective, which provides a dedicated set of tools for managing models and metamodels.

You can select the **Modeling** perspective by navigating to **Window → Perspective → Open Perspective →

Modeling**.

- **Model Explorer View**: The **Model Explorer** is an essential component for working with EMF and VIATRA. It provides a structured view of models and metamodels, allowing easy navigation between classes, relationships, and properties.

Activate this view by going to **Window → Show View → Other → Modeling → Model Explorer**.

- **Window Organization**: Arrange your workspace by strategically dividing windows. For example, place the **Model Explorer** on the left side, the code editor in the center, and the **Console** or **Problem View** at the bottom to monitor errors or warnings when running queries and transformations.

1.3. Eclipse Modeling Framework (EMF) Support

As mentioned earlier, VIATRA relies on EMF, a modeling framework that allows you to define and manage models and metamodels. Before using VIATRA, it's crucial to properly configure EMF support:

1. **Creating an EMF Project**:

   - Go to **File → New → Project**.

   - Select **Ecore Modeling Project** to create a new project based on EMF.

   - Set the project name and follow the prompts to configure the Ecore model.

2. **Ecore Diagram Editor**: Eclipse provides a graphical editor to create Ecore diagrams, simplifying the definition of metamodels. You can create and visualize classes, attributes, and relationships between classes directly in a diagram.

1.4. Integration with Other Modeling

Tools

VIATRA can be used in combination with other modeling tools available in Eclipse, such as Papyrus and Xtext, to further enhance your workspace.

- **Papyrus**: Papyrus is a graphical modeling tool that supports UML (Unified Modeling Language) and SysML (Systems Modeling Language). You can use it alongside VIATRA to create UML models and define transformations on them.

- **Xtext**: If you need to create domain-specific languages, you can integrate VIATRA with Xtext. Xtext allows you to create new programming or modeling languages with a dedicated editor, and you can use VIATRA to write transformations on the models defined in your custom languages.

---

2. Customizations

Customizing Queries in VIATRA

One of VIATRA's key features is the ability to define custom queries to search for specific models. Using the VIATRA Query Language (VQL), you can tailor queries to suit your specific needs.

2.1. Writing Custom Queries

Custom queries can be written to identify specific models within a project. Here is an example of a custom query that finds all courses with more than 50 students:

```vql
pattern crowdedCourses(course: Course) {
```

```
    Course(course);

    count find studentsInCourse(_, course) > 50;

}
```
```

In this query:

- `Course(course)` identifies all instances of the `Course` class.

- The `count find` function counts the number of students enrolled in each course and returns only those with more than 50 students.

##### 2.2. Using Logical Constraints in Queries

You can further customize queries by using logical constraints to refine the results. For example, you can write a query that finds all professors who teach both math and computer
```

science courses:

```vql
pattern versatileProfessors(professor: Professor) {
    Professor(professor);
    find teachesCourse(professor, "Mathematics");
    find teachesCourse(professor, "Computer Science");
}
```

This query returns only professors who teach both "Mathematics" and "Computer Science."

Customizing Transformations

In addition to queries, transformations in VIATRA can be customized to fit specific scenarios.

2.3. Defining Conditional Transformation Rules

Transformations can be written to apply changes to models based on certain conditions. Here's an example of a transformation rule that automatically assigns a tutor to a student only if the student is enrolled in more than five courses:

```java
rule assignTutorToStudent {
    from
        student: Student
    where {
        count find studentCourses(student, _) > 5;
    }
```

```
    to {
        var tutor = new Tutor;
        student.tutor = tutor;
        tutor.name = "Tutor for " + student.name;
    }
}
```

This transformation rule assigns a tutor to the student and updates the model based on dynamic conditions.

---

3. Debugging Tools

Debugging VIATRA Queries

One of the most important aspects of

integrating VIATRA with Eclipse is debugging queries and transformations. Eclipse offers a variety of tools that can be used to debug models, queries, and transformation rules.

3.1. Debugging VQL Queries

The VIATRA Query Language (VQL) has debugging support tools that allow you to verify query results and troubleshoot issues.

1. **Using the VIATRA Console**: The **VIATRA Console** can be used to manually execute queries and view results. You can access the console through **Window → Show View → Other → VIATRA Query Console**.

2. **Breakpoints in Queries**: You can set breakpoints in VIATRA queries to pause execution at specific points and inspect partial results. This is especially useful when

working with complex queries that involve multiple models or conditions.

3. **Query Performance Analysis**: VIATRA includes tools for analyzing query performance. You can use performance analysis to identify slow or inefficient queries and optimize them.

By integrating VIATRA into your Eclipse workspace, you can maximize your modeling and transformation capabilities.

5. Practical Examples of Eclipse VIATRA

Eclipse VIATRA is a powerful tool for pattern matching and model transformation, widely used in real-world applications to solve complex problems in the field of modeling and model-based systems. In this article, we will explore some practical and detailed examples of using Eclipse VIATRA for **pattern matching**, **model transformation**, and some **real-world applications** where this tool is used.

Example of Pattern Matching in Eclipse VIATRA

Pattern matching is a core feature of VIATRA, allowing users to search for specific elements within a model. With VIATRA, you can define patterns that specify the structure of the elements to be found and then run the search using the pattern matching engine.

1. Model Definition

Before starting with the pattern matching example, you need a model. Let's assume we are working with a simplified model of a **university** containing classes like `Course`, `Student`, and `Professor`. Here's what the metamodel in Ecore might look like:

- **Course**: has a name and a list of enrolled students.

- **Student**: has a name and a list of courses they are enrolled in.

- **Professor**: has a name and a list of courses they teach.

2. Creating a VIATRA Project

1. Open Eclipse and create a new EMF project

named "UniversityModel."

2. Define your Ecore model to represent the university. In Eclipse, you can create the Ecore model using a diagram editor. Add the classes `Course`, `Student`, and `Professor` and the respective relationships between them.

3. Defining the Pattern Matching

Once the model is ready, we can create a VIATRA query to execute pattern matching. The goal of this example will be to find all courses with more than 50 enrolled students.

Pattern Matching Query

VIATRA uses its own query language called **VIATRA Query Language** (VQL). The following VQL query looks for all courses with more than 50 students:

```vql
package university.queries

pattern crowdedCourses(course: Course) {
    Course(course);
    count find studentsInCourse(_, course) > 50;
}

pattern studentsInCourse(student: Student, course: Course) {
    Student.courses(student, course);
}
```

Query Explanation

- The `crowdedCourses` query looks for instances of the `Course` class that have more than 50 students.

- The `studentsInCourse` query is used as part of the first query to count how many students are enrolled in each course.

- The `count find` function is used to count the number of students associated with each course.

Running the Query

To run this query:

1. Go to the **Viatra Query Explorer** view in Eclipse.

2. Load your university model into the query engine.

3. Execute the `crowdedCourses` query.

The result will be a list of courses with more than 50 students, which will be displayed in the VIATRA Query console.

4. Complex Queries

VIATRA queries can easily be extended to include more complex constraints. For example, we can extend the query to find all courses with more than 50 students taught by a specific professor.

```vql
pattern crowdedCoursesWithProfessor(course: Course, professor: Professor) {
    Course(course);
    Professor.courses(professor, course);
    count find studentsInCourse(_, course) > 50;
}
```

In this case, the query searches for crowded

courses taught by a particular professor.

Model Transformation

Model transformation is another key feature of VIATRA. Transformation rules allow you to modify an existing model or transform it into another model following predefined rules. In this example, we will see how to create a transformation that automatically assigns a tutor to students enrolled in more than five courses.

1. Defining Transformation Rules

Transformation rules in VIATRA can be defined using the **Viatra Transformation Language** (VTL). Let's assume you want to automate the assignment of a tutor to overloaded students, meaning students enrolled in more than five courses.

Transformation Rule

Here is a simple transformation rule that assigns a tutor to all students enrolled in more than five courses:

```java
rule assignTutor {
    from
        student: Student
    where {
        count find studentCourses(student, _) > 5;
    }
    to {
        tutor = new Tutor;
        student.tutor = tutor;
```

```
        tutor.name = "Tutor for " + student.name;
  }
}
```

Rule Explanation

- **Condition (from)**: The transformation selects all students in the model.

- **Constraint (where)**: The condition `count find studentCourses(student, _) > 5` specifies that the transformation applies only to students enrolled in more than five courses.

- **Action (to)**: The transformation creates a new instance of the `Tutor` class and assigns it to the student. Additionally, the tutor's name is dynamically generated based on the student's name.

2. Executing the Transformation

To execute this transformation:

1. Load the student model into the transformation engine.

2. Run the `assignTutor` rule.

The result will be that every student enrolled in more than five courses will have a tutor assigned. You can verify the results by updating the model view in Eclipse.

3. Incremental Transformations

VIATRA also supports incremental transformations, meaning that transformations can be applied in real-time as models change. For example, if a new student is added to the model and enrolls in six courses, the transformation rule can automatically assign a tutor without manually rerunning the transformation.

Real-World Applications of Eclipse VIATRA

Eclipse VIATRA has been used in various real-world contexts to solve complex problems related to modeling, pattern matching, and model transformation. Below are some examples of real-world applications where VIATRA has proven its effectiveness.

1. Real-Time Monitoring Systems

One of the primary applications of VIATRA is in real-time monitoring systems. VIATRA is used to monitor dynamic models and detect changes in real-time. A typical example is the use of VIATRA in industrial automation systems, where models represent the state of machinery and production processes.

Example: Production Monitoring

In a manufacturing plant, VIATRA can be used to monitor models representing machines and their operations. When a machine reports an error or failure, VIATRA can trigger a transformation that automatically sends a notification to operators and updates the model to reflect the machine's error state.

```vql
pattern faultyMachines(machine: Machine) {
    Machine(machine);
    machine.status == "ERROR";
}
```

The `faultyMachines` query detects all machines with an error status, and a subsequent transformation can send notifications or trigger maintenance procedures.

2. Model-Based Design Systems

VIATRA is often used in model-based design systems, where model transformation is a key requirement. For example, VIATRA can be used in a software design system to automatically transform UML models into source code.

Example: Automatic Code Generation from UML Models

In a UML-based software design environment, UML models can be transformed into Java code using transformation rules written in VIATRA.

```java
rule generateJavaClass {
```

```
    from
        class: UMLClass
    to {
        javaClass = new JavaClass;
        javaClass.name = class.name;
        // Transform attributes and methods
    }
}
```

This transformation reads a UML class and automatically generates a corresponding Java class with the same name.

3. Network Model Optimization

Another common application of VIATRA is optimizing network models in network engineering scenarios. For instance, VIATRA can be used to optimize the configuration of sensor networks or communication networks based on models.

Example: Sensor Network Optimization

In a sensor network, VIATRA can be used to monitor the links between sensors and optimize the network topology. The following query detects redundant links between sensors:

```vql
pattern redundantLinks(sensor1: Sensor, sensor2: Sensor) {
    Sensor.links(sensor1, sensor2);
    find nearbySensor(sensor1, sensor2);
}
```

A subsequent transformation can remove

redundant links to optimize the network.

6.Troubleshooting Eclipse VIATRA

Eclipse VIATRA is a powerful and complex tool for handling models, transformations, and pattern matching, but like any advanced software, you may encounter several issues while using it. This article explores the **most common problems** that can arise when working with Eclipse VIATRA, provides **detailed solutions** to these issues, and offers practical examples for resolving them. Whether you're working with complex models, optimizing pattern matching, or configuring transformations, having a troubleshooting guide will help you work more efficiently.

---

1. Installation and Configuration Issues

Issue 1: Eclipse VIATRA is not installed correctly

Symptom: After following the installation steps, Eclipse VIATRA does not appear among the available options, or the VIATRA features seem incomplete.

Common causes:

- Incompatible Eclipse versions.

- Missing or incorrectly installed components.

- Connection issues during package download.

Solution:

1. **Check Eclipse version**: VIATRA requires a specific version of Eclipse. Make sure your Eclipse version is compatible with the version of VIATRA you are trying to install. VIATRA works best with the Eclipse IDE for Modeling Tools. You can download the correct version of Eclipse from the [official Eclipse website] (https://www.eclipse.org/).

2. **Reload VIATRA packages**: If the components did not load properly, try reinstalling the VIATRA plugin by following these steps:

   - Go to **Help** -> **Eclipse Marketplace**.

   - Search for "VIATRA" in the search bar and reinstall the plugin.

   - Ensure that you have installed all necessary packages (e.g., EMF, Xtext, and VIATRA Query).

3. **Connection issues**: If you suspect connection problems during the download, you can manually download the VIATRA packages and install them through **Install New Software** by entering the VIATRA repository URL: `http://download.eclipse.org/viatra/releases/latest`.

Issue 2: Incorrect EMF project configuration

Symptom: Errors during code generation from the Ecore model or failure to run queries on the created models.

Common causes:

- Errors in the Ecore model definition.

- Missing or misconfigured Ecore or GenModel files.

- Missing dependencies in the project.

Solution:

1. **Validate the Ecore model**: Ensure that the Ecore model is correct. Go to **Validate** to check for any structural errors in your model. Resolve any errors before proceeding.

2. **Generate the code**: After creating the Ecore model, you need to correctly generate the model code:

- Right-click on the `.genmodel` file and select **Generate Model Code**.

   - Ensure that all classes and objects are generated without errors.

3. **Verify dependencies**: Add any missing dependencies. If your project uses VIATRA and other tools like EMF, make sure the dependencies are correctly configured in the `MANIFEST.MF` file or the build file.

---

2. Pattern Matching Issues

Issue 3: The query returns no results

Symptom: After executing a pattern matching query, no results are returned, even though you are certain there are matches in the model.

Common causes:

- Errors in the pattern definition.

- Mismatch between the pattern and the model.

- Errors in loading the model into the pattern matching engine.

Solution:

1. **Check the pattern definition**: Ensure that the pattern is correctly defined in the `.vql` file. Verify the syntax and that the variables are properly declared and used. For example, in a query like this:

```vql
pattern crowdedCourses(course: Course) {
    Course(course);
    count find studentsInCourse(_, course) > 50;
```

}
```

Verify that the class name `Course` and the fields match exactly with those defined in your Ecore model.

2. **Ensure the model is loaded**: Confirm that the model on which you're performing pattern matching is correctly loaded into the VIATRA engine. You can check this from the **Viatra Query Explorer**:

   - Go to **Viatra Query Explorer** -> **Load Model** and ensure that your model is visible and loaded.

3. **Use query debugging**: Eclipse VIATRA offers tools for debugging queries. You can set **breakpoints** in the queries to see where the pattern matching engine fails. Use the **VIATRA Query Console** to manually run queries and inspect partial results.
```

Issue 4: Duplicate results in queries

Symptom: The pattern matching query returns duplicate or overlapping results.

Common causes:

- Incorrect variable or context definition in the pattern.

- Lack of specific constraints in the pattern.

Solution:

1. **Check pattern variables**: Ensure that the variables in the pattern are correctly defined and that there are no unnecessary repetitions. For example, in a query that searches for relationships between students and courses, duplicates might occur if constraints are not properly defined.

2. **Add constraints**: If you receive

duplicate results, you may need to add constraints to narrow down the pattern. Here is an example of a query that uses an additional constraint to avoid duplicates:

```vql
pattern coursesWithUniqueStudents(course: Course, student: Student) {
    Course(course);
    Student.courses(student, course);
    // Add a constraint to avoid duplicates
    not find duplicateStudent(student);
}
```

Here, the pattern uses the `not find` constraint to exclude students who may appear multiple times in the results.

---

3. Transformation Rule Issues

Issue 5: Transformation rules not executing

Symptom: Despite defining the transformation rules correctly, the model does not change after running the transformation.

Common causes:

- Error in defining the rule activation conditions.

- Transformation rules not applied correctly.

Solution:

1. **Check activation conditions**: Make sure the conditions specified in the transformation rules are correct. For example, if you have a rule that triggers only when a course has more than 50 students, verify that

this condition is indeed met in the model.

2. **Use the transformation console**: VIATRA provides a **transformation console** that allows you to see which rules are being applied and when. Ensure that the rule is being triggered and that the condition is satisfied.

3. **Run the transformation manually**: Try manually running the transformation rule to see if it works. For example, use a debugger to step through the transformation and see if the model changes as expected.

Issue 6: Models not updated after transformation

Symptom: Even though the transformation runs successfully, the changes are not reflected in the original model.

Common causes:

- Synchronization issues between the transformation engine and the model.

- Errors in committing changes to the model.

Solution:

1. **Ensure changes are committed**: Make sure that changes made by the transformation engine are applied to the model and not just held in memory. VIATRA can support incremental synchronization, so ensure this feature is enabled if you want to see changes in real time.

2. **Reload the model**: Sometimes the model view might not be updated immediately after a transformation. Try reloading the model in the **Model Explorer** to view the changes.

---

4. Performance Issues

Issue 7: Slow or inefficient pattern matching

Symptom: Pattern matching query execution is slow, especially on large models.

Common causes:

- Models too large to be processed efficiently.

- Poorly optimized or complex patterns.

Solution:

1. **Optimize queries**: VIATRA queries can be optimized by using more specific constraints to reduce the number of elements the engine has to match. For example, if you are looking for relationships between very general classes, narrow the constraints by adding more conditions in the pattern:

```vql
pattern coursesWithFewStudents(course: Course) {
    Course(course);
    count find studentsInCourse(_, course) < 10;
}
```

This query narrows the search to courses with fewer than 10 students, reducing the load on the query engine.

2. **Use caching**: VIATRA supports **result caching** to avoid repeatedly running the same query on large models. Configure caching to improve performance for recurring queries.

Issue 8: High memory consumption

Symptom: Eclipse VIATRA consumes a large amount of memory during complex query or transformation execution.

Common causes:

- Queries generating too many results.

- Transformations creating too many instances or modifying large portions of the model.

Solution:

1. **Optimize transformation rules**: Avoid creating new instances or modifying the model excessively in a single transformation rule. For example, if a transformation must modify many objects, try splitting the work into multiple rules.

2. **Incrementality**: If working with very large models, take advantage of VIATRA's query incrementalization. This means that queries are only executed on modified parts of the model, significantly reducing memory consumption.

7. Glossary of Eclipse VIATRA

Eclipse VIATRA is a powerful and versatile platform for query-based model transformation and management, with a focus on pattern matching and model transformations in complex contexts. To better understand the key concepts and terminology used in VIATRA, it is helpful to have an overview of the main terms. Below is a comprehensive glossary with detailed definitions covering the fundamental concepts of Eclipse VIATRA.

Integrated Development Environment (IDE)

An IDE is software that provides comprehensive tools for application development, including code editors, compilers, and debugging tools. Eclipse is a widely-used IDE for Java-based software development, and VIATRA functions as an extension of Eclipse, adding capabilities for modeling and transformation.

API (Application Programming Interface)

An API is a set of tools and definitions that enables communication between software components. VIATRA provides APIs to interact with the pattern matching engine and to define transformation rules.

Automated Transformations

The process of automatically transforming models according to predefined rules. In VIATRA, these transformations can be used to automate the management and updating of models.

Match

A match in VIATRA refers to a single instance of a pattern found in a model. If a pattern specifies a certain structure or relationship, a match represents an occurrence of that structure in the model.

EMF (Eclipse Modeling Framework)

EMF is an Eclipse platform for modeling that allows developers to define structural models and generate code. VIATRA uses EMF to work with Ecore models.

Ecore

The metamodeling language of EMF. Ecore allows the definition of conceptual models that describe data structure and constraints. In VIATRA, patterns and transformations operate on Ecore models.

Incremental Execution

A technique used by VIATRA to optimize query processing. Instead of running queries on the entire model, incremental execution allows updating only the results when the model changes, greatly improving efficiency.

Filter

In VIATRA, a filter is an additional condition that can be applied to patterns to narrow down query results. For example, a filter could specify that only objects of a certain type should be considered in a match.

Model Generation

The process of automatically creating a model from another model or a metamodel specification. VIATRA supports automatic model generation through transformation rules.

Inference

The process of deducing new information based on existing data and transformation rules in models. Inference enables the enrichment of models with new relationships or structures.

Instance

An instance in a model is a concrete example of an element defined in the metamodel. If the metamodel defines a class "Person," an instance of "Person" could be an individual with specific attributes.

Query Interpreter

A component of VIATRA that executes queries on models and returns pattern-matching results. The query engine examines the model and searches for instances that satisfy the conditions defined in the patterns.

Java Development Tools (JDT)

A set of tools in Eclipse for developing Java applications. VIATRA integrates with Eclipse and its Java Development Tools, making it possible to manage and transform models directly within Eclipse.

Pattern Matching Engine

VIATRA's engine that executes queries to search for specific patterns within models. It uses a combination of optimization techniques to improve efficiency, especially in large-scale models.

Metamodel

A metamodel is a model that describes the structure of other models. In VIATRA, metamodels are defined using Ecore. They specify the classes, attributes, and relationships that can be used in concrete models.

Model

A model is a representation of a system or concept in terms of objects and relationships. VIATRA works on models defined in EMF, which can represent complex systems in various domains.

Pattern

A pattern in VIATRA is a specific structure or relationship that needs to be searched within a model. Patterns can describe configurations of objects and relationships that should be found, such as "all courses with more than 50 students."

Pattern Matching

The process of finding matches for a specific pattern within a model. VIATRA is designed to perform efficient pattern matching, even in complex or large models.

Plug-in

A plug-in is a software extension that adds functionality to an existing platform. Eclipse VIATRA is a plug-in for Eclipse that adds pattern matching and model transformation capabilities.

Query

A query in VIATRA is a request that specifies a pattern to be searched for in a model. Queries are expressed using the VIATRA Query Language (VQL) and can be executed to retrieve information from the model.

Transformation Rule

Transformation rules define how to modify or create a model based on another model. In VIATRA, these rules can be applied automatically to transform models according to defined constraints.

VIATRA Repository

The VIATRA repository is a collection of software packages from which the latest versions of VIATRA and its dependencies can be downloaded. Users can configure Eclipse to download and update VIATRA directly from this repository.

Dependency Network

VIATRA can build a dependency network that tracks relationships between objects and query results in the model. This allows only the affected parts of the model to be updated, improving performance.

Incremental Result

An incremental result refers to the way query results are automatically updated when the model changes. This is particularly useful for dynamic models where data may frequently be modified.

Rule-based Transformation

A rule-based transformation in VIATRA is one where specific rules describe how and when the model should be modified. Rules can be executed automatically or manually in response to specific events.

Incremental Synchronization

A feature of VIATRA that allows synchronizing models incrementally, updating only the parts that have changed rather than the entire model. This approach greatly improves performance in complex scenarios.

Model-Driven System

A model-driven system uses models as the primary source of specifications and implementations for applications. In such a system, VIATRA can be used to efficiently manage and transform models.

Persistent Terms

Terms that refer to data or information that can be stored and maintained outside of volatile memory, such as models stored in XML files or databases. VIATRA can operate on persistent models by loading them into memory and applying its operations.

Model Transformation

The process of modifying or generating a model from another model. VIATRA supports this process through transformation rules and pattern matching, facilitating the evolution and updating of models.

Viatra Query Explorer

A component of the Eclipse IDE that allows

interactive exploration and management of VIATRA queries. Developers can run queries, view results, and inspect matches directly within Eclipse.

VIATRA Query Language (VQL)

A query language used in VIATRA to define patterns and queries on models. VQL provides an expressive syntax for searching structures and relationships within EMF models.

Workspace

The workspace in Eclipse is the working environment that contains projects, models, and configurations. VIATRA operates within the Eclipse workspace, integrating with other modeling tools.

This glossary provides an overview of the key concepts and terms of Eclipse VIATRA, offering a solid foundation for understanding how this platform works and how to use it effectively for pattern matching and model transformation. Understanding these terms facilitates the use of VIATRA and allows for optimal use of its capabilities in managing complex models.

Index

1. Introduction to Eclipse VIATRA pg.4

2. Fundamental Concepts of Eclipse VIATRA pg.16

3. Using Eclipse VIATRA pg.34

4. Integration with Eclipse VIATRA pg.47

5. Practical Examples of Eclipse VIATRA pg.61

6. Troubleshooting Eclipse VIATRA pg.77

7. Glossary of Eclipse VIATRA pg.92

www.ingramcontent.com/pod-product-compliance
Lightning Source LLC
Chambersburg PA
CBHW071101240526
45471CB00016B/2296